A New True Book

THAILAND

By Karen Jacobsen

Flag of Thailand

CHILDRENS PRESS®

CHICAGO

Temple of Dawn,
Bangkok, Thailand

PHOTO CREDITS

AP/Wide World Photos—17 (left), 28

© Cameramann International Ltd.—9 (right), 10, 13 (right), 14, 15 (right), 19 (top and bottom right), 33, 36 (2 photos), 37 (2 photos), 38 (right), 39 (left), 41, 42, 43

© Joan Dunlop—8, 11 (left), 19 (bottom left), 21, 35 (left)

The Marilyn Gartman Agency—© Christy Volpe, 29

Grolier Incorporated—4 (map)

Historical Pictures Service, Chicago—23 (2 photos), 24 (2 photos)

JIG—© Betty Groskin, 6 (inset), 45

Nawrocki Stock Photo—© Ulrike Welsch, 11 (right), 26; © D. K. Hulcher, 35 (right)

Odyssey Productions—© Robert Frerck, 16

Chip and Rosa Maria de la Cueva Peterson—© Don & Meg Arnosti, 17 (right), 19 (top left)

Photo Source International—4 (bottom)

Photri—7, 31 (top), 38 (left); © ABY, 15 (left); © Spillane, 27

Roloc Color Slides—31 (top)

Root Resources—© Kenneth W. Fink, 9 (left)

Shostal Associates—32 (right); © David Muscroft, 2; © Herbert Lanks, 6 (top); © Giorgio Ricatto, 13 (left); © Manley Photo-Tuscon, Ariz, Cover, 31 (bottom); © D. J. Forbert, 39 (right)

Tony Stone Worldwide-Click/Chicago—32 (left); © Karen Philips, 40

Len Meents maps—8, 12, 13, 14

Cover — Gateway of Wat Arun, Bangkok

Library of Congress Cataloging-in-Publication Data

Jacobsen, Karen.
    Thailand / by Karen Jacobsen.
        p.   cm. — (A New true book)
    Includes index.
    Summary: Introduces the history, land, people, religion, and culture of this exotic country in Southeast Asia.
    ISBN 0-516-01179-0
    1. Thailand—Juvenile literature. [1. Thailand.]
I. Title.
DS563.5.J23   1989
959.3—dc20   89-34413
                                         CIP
                                          AC

TABLE OF CONTENTS

Village in rural Thailand

THE LAND

Thailand is in Southeast Asia. Many people think that on a map the shape of Thailand looks like the shape of an elephant's head. Its forehead leans against Burma, now called Myanmar. Its ears touch Laos and Cambodia, also known as Kampuchea. Its long, thin trunk reaches down between the Gulf of Thailand and the Andaman Sea to the Malay Peninsula.

Today elephants are trained to do heavy work. Elephants have a special place in Thailand. Visitors to the Grand Palace in Bangkok may see bushes shaped like elephants (left).

Elephants have always been important in Thailand. Long ago, they lived in wild herds. Later, Thai warriors trained young elephants for use in battle.

Beautiful beaches and fruit trees are found in southern Thailand.

Thailand is a beautiful country. It has four parts: the northwest mountains, the northeast plateau, the southern peninsula, and the central plains. Each part is different from the others.

THE NORTHWEST MOUNTAINS

Hmong village in the northern mountains

Most of northwestern Thailand is covered with forests, high hills, and mountains. The highest, Inthanon Mountain, rises 8,514 feet. Teak trees and evergreen trees grow in the forests. The wood from Thailand's forests is shipped all over the world.

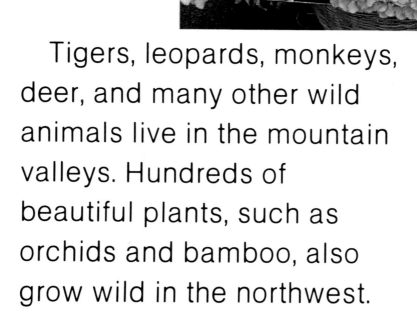

The clouded leopard (above) lives in the forest. Offerings of orchids, strings of flowers, or carved wooden elephants are made at temples throughout Thailand.

Tigers, leopards, monkeys, deer, and many other wild animals live in the mountain valleys. Hundreds of beautiful plants, such as orchids and bamboo, also grow wild in the northwest.

This Paka villager and his horses live in the mountains.

Not many people live in
the mountains. Most
mountain people still live in
tribes and follow the old
ways. They raise livestock
and grow fruit, vegetables,

and rice in small fields near their villages.

Chiang Mai is the main city in the northwest. People come from all over the world to buy the arts and crafts made in Chiang Mai.

The city of Chiang Mai (left) and Phu Ping Palace (right), the summer home of the royal family

THE NORTHEAST AND THE SOUTH

Bangkok

Northeastern Thailand is a flat and sandy plateau. Its soil is not good for farming. For most of the year the northeast is dry. But sometimes there is too much rain and the Mekong River overflows and floods the land.

The southern part of Thailand shares the Malay Peninsula with Myanmar (Burma) and Malaysia. Southern

A beach in Thailand (left),
and a road through
the rain forest (above)

Thailand has mountains, jungles, and white sandy beaches. Its humid, rainy climate is perfect for growing trees and tropical fruits, such as coconuts and bananas. But not many people live there.

Bangkok
★

A farmer's home stands in a field of rice seedlings.

CENTRAL THAILAND

Bangkok

Most of the country's 56 million people live in central Thailand. From the northern mountains to the Gulf of Thailand, this land is among the best farmland in the world. Enough rice is grown

Thai workers plant and harvest rice by hand.

on the central plains to feed
all of Thailand's people.

Thailand depends on the
Chao Phraya River.
Thousands of irrigation
ditches carry the river water
to the rice fields. The Chao
Phraya is also a river road.

15

The Chao Phraya River cuts through Bangkok.

It carries the Thai people and their goods from one place to another.

Bangkok, Thailand's capital and largest city, is near the mouth of the Chao Phraya River. Nearly six million people live in

Traffic flows past Democracy Monument on Rajdamnoen Avenue (left) in Bangkok. The klong people of Bangkok do their shopping by boat (right). They go fishing, wash clothes, and bathe in the river.

Bangkok. Many people live in boats along the river or on its many canals, called klongs.

Bangkok is a modern city. It is a world center for trade, banking, and tourism. Bangkok attracts people who want to make money.

17

THE PEOPLE

The first Thai people came south from China and moved into the central region. Other tribes already lived there, but the Thai were stronger and took over.

Today, most people in Thailand are Thai. But there are now also members of the Khmer, Mon, and other tribes, as well as Malays, Indians, Chinese, Japanese, and Europeans.

Black-turbaned Hmong woman with her baby (above left), young man from northern Thailand (above right), female construction workers (below left), and a young family (below right) are all a part of Thailand today.

LONG AGO IN THAILAND

The first Thai kingdom
began in 1238 A.D. Its early
kings were warriors. They
fought battles to protect
their kingdom from outside
enemies. But they also
brought scholars and skilled
workers from China and India
to teach the Thai people.
The Thai kingdom grew.

By 1350, Ayutthaya, a city
on the Chao Phraya River,
had become the Thai
capital. During the next 400

The ruins of the city of Ayutthaya

years, the Thais made laws,
collected taxes, and grew
stronger. They traded with
China, India, and other
countries as far away as
Europe. They built fine
homes and many beautiful

temples. They fought and won wars against invaders from Burma and Cambodia.

But, in 1767, the Burmese army invaded and destroyed the city of Ayutthaya. Fifteen years later, a new city was started across the river at Bangkok. There, in 1782, Rama I became the first king of Siam, the new name for the Thai kingdom.

Over the next 150 years, the kings of Siam led their people. They brought new inventions and modern ways of thinking to Siam. They kept their country strong and free from foreign powers.

KINGS OF SIAM	
Rama II (1809-1824)	poet, scholar; kept peace
Rama III (1824-1851)	feared foreign takeover; limited trade with the West; allowed Christian missionaries into the country
Mongkut Rama IV (1851-1868)	Buddhist monk, scholar (knew Latin, English, mathematics history, geography); encouraged education and modern development
Chulalongkorn Rama V (1868-1910)	abolished slavery; encouraged modernization; loved by Thai people. The anniversary of his death is a national holiday in Thailand.
Vajiravudh Rama VI (1910-1925)	encouraged international role for Siam; joined Red Cross and the Boy Scouts; fought with the Allies against Germany in World War I
Prajadhipok Rama VII (1925-1935)	was forced to rule under Constitution from 1932 until 1935 when he gave up the throne

Mongkut, Rama IV (above) and Chulalongkorn, Rama V (below)

Chulalongkorn, Rama V, presents his son, Crown Prince Vajiravudh, who later became Rama VI, to the people. Prajadhipok, Rama VII, (right) was forced to give up his throne.

Rama VII became king in 1925. Some Thai leaders did not like the way he ran the country. In 1932, they forced Rama VII to give up his power. New leaders took charge of Siam.

LAND OF THE FREE

In 1939, the name of the country was changed to Muang Thai. The name means "land of the free" in the Thai language.

But, only two years later, Thailand lost its freedom. The Japanese army invaded and took over the government.

Then, in 1945, Japan was defeated. Thai leaders again took charge. A new king, Bhumibol, was crowned

Bhumibol, Rama IX,
is the king of Thailand.
The king has little power,
but most Thais respect
the king and his family.

Rama IX, king of Thailand.
Since the war, Thailand
has been run by military
leaders. There is a
Constitution and the prime
minister is the head of
government. The king gives
advice to the prime minister
and appears at important
events.

THAILAND TODAY

Fleeing war in their own countries, refugees seek safety in Thailand.

Thailand is at peace, but for many years its neighbors in Vietnam, Myanmar (Burma), Laos, and Cambodia (Kampuchea) have been at war. Hundreds of thousands of people have been killed. Thousands of refugees have moved into Thailand for safety. The Thais want the fighting to stop. They want

the peaceful development
of Southeast Asia to begin.

For two hundred years the
Grand Palace in Bangkok
has been the home of
Thailand's kings. Covering a
square-mile area along the
banks of the Chao Phraya, it

The Grand Palace in Bangkok has many buildings and temples within its walls.

The king and his family live in this building within the Grand Palace.

is a city within a city. Many public events are held at the Grand Palace.

Within the walls of the Grand Palace, there are several beautiful Buddhist monasteries (wats) and

temples (bots). Hundreds
more can be visited in other
parts of Bangkok. There are
thousands more around the
country. Buddhist wats are
guarded by statues of
demons, or elephants, or
other animals.

All Thai temples honor
Buddha, the founder of the
Buddhist religion. Buddha
taught people to gain
personal peace by thinking
peaceful thoughts.

Wat Po Temple (above) is also known as the Temple of the Thousand Buddhas. The Temple of the Emerald Buddha (below) is decorated with gold and jewels.

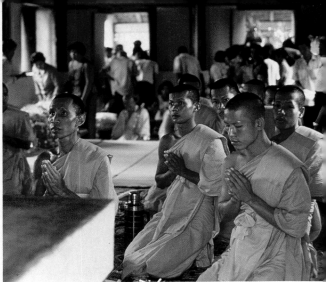

Young Buddhists study the teachings of
Buddha in wats and temples throughout Thailand.

Many young men become
Buddhist monks for a few
months or longer. They live
simple lives and study their
religion. People think it is an
honor to give food to the
monks. It is a way to "make
merit," to do a good deed.
Buddhists try to do good
32   deeds as often as possible.

Spirit houses are everywhere.

It is the custom in Thailand to put spirit houses outside homes and along roadways. The Thais place food, flowers, and incense in the small houses—to please the spirits that live nearby. The Thais believe that happy spirits will not cause trouble. **33**

LIFE IN THAILAND

Thais celebrate many holidays. Songkran, in early April, is the beginning of the Thai New Year. People swim in rivers and throw water at each other to wash away bad luck. Loi Krathong is held on the night of the full moon in October or in November. People light candles in little flower-filled baskets and float them on the river. The baskets are

A Loi Krathong basket (left). During Songkran people throw water at one another to wash away bad luck.

meant to carry away all troubles.

Thailand has a rich tradition of legends and storytelling. Thai stories are told in plays and in dances. The performers wear costumes

Young dancers and musicans keep
the traditional dances (left)
and music of Thailand alive.

stitched with gold and
jewels. Their headdresses
are made to look like Thai
temples. Every movement of
their bodies carries a special
meaning. The music, played
on flutes, gongs, and drums,
helps to tell the story.

In Thailand, boxers (left)
fight with their feet, too.
Villagers use special nets (above)
to catch fish.

Thais enjoy sports. For
many, ballgames, swimming,
boating, and fishing are part
of everyday life. Thais love
to gamble. They bet on the
lottery and on contests of
all kinds, from fighting fish
to kick-boxing matches.

Kite-flying is a popular sport
throughout Thailand.

Kite-flying is another
favorite Thai sport. The
contest is between two
flying kites. Each kite has
powdered glass glued on its
string. The kite flyers try to
cut each other's kite string.
The kite that falls first
becomes the prize of the
other kite flyer.

CRAFTS

Thai craftspeople make
paper into kites, parasols,
flowers, and other products.
Clothing and other beautiful
products are made from
Thai silk.

Traditional designs
are painted on a
paper and bamboo
umbrella (left) and are
woven into
silk fabric (above).

Master carvers use teak
and other woods to create
sculptures of Thai heroes,
story characters, and animals.
Thai children work with the
adults to learn the family craft.
Throughout Thailand,
children work next to their
parents on farms, in the
forests, and on the waterways.

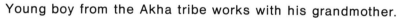

Young boy from the Akha tribe works with his grandmother.

SCHOOLS

In modern Thailand, education for all Thais has become very important.

The government is training more teachers. For the first time, in villages far from Bangkok, young children are

Primary school in an Akha village

King Ramkhamhaeng developed the Thai alphabet and writing system.

learning to read and write.

From age eight to fourteen, students may go to free schools. But high school costs money. Most Thai children are poor. So only about one student in ten is able to stay in school.

Thailand has 14 universities, more than 43 teachers' colleges, and 170 vocational schools. Every year, more Thai students graduate and take their place in Thailand's government and business life.

Chulalongkorn University in Bangkok

THAILAND IS CHANGING

Many people in Thailand
live very much as the Thai
people did more than a
hundred years ago. Change
happens very slowly in Thailand.

But change is happening.
The king and the government
are building schools and
improving health care. They
are developing new industries

Students are bringing more changes to Thailand.

to create more and better jobs.
Today in Thailand the old
ways remain and are valued.
But at the same time, the
people are learning new
skills. Thailand is becoming
a modern country.

WORDS YOU SHOULD KNOW

allies(AL • eyes) — people or nations united for a cause

Asia(AY • jah) — the largest continent on earth

Buddha(BOO • da) — a religious leader who lived in India about 2,500 years ago

Buddhism(BOO • diz • im) — the religion started by Buddha

Buddhist(BOO • dist) — a person who follows the religion of Buddhism

canal(kuh • NAL) — a constructed water channel

capital(CAP • ih • til) — the place where a country's government is located

constitution(kahn • sti • TOO • shun) — a system of basic laws or rules for the government of a country

demon(DEE • mun) — an evil spirit

foreign(FOR • in) — of or from another country

gulf(GUHLF) — an arm of the sea

humid(HYOO • mid) — damp, moist

incense(IN • sense) — a material that gives off perfume when burned

irrigation(ir • ih • GAY • shun) — supplying water to crops by a system of pipes or ditches

invade(in • VAID) — to enter for war or conquest

legend(LEH • jend) — a story from the past

livestock(LYVE • stahk) — animals raised for food, hides, feathers, or fur

lottery(LOT • er • ee) — the selection of numbered tickets for the awarding of prizes; a random drawing

monastery(MAHN • is • ter • ee) — a residence for monks or other religious groups

monk(MUNK) — a man who lives in a religious house and follows certain rules

Myanmar(myan • MAH) — the name for the country formerly known as Burma.

native(NAY • tihv) — born in or belonging to a place
parasol(PAR • uh • sawl) — an umbrellalike shade for the sun
peninsula(pen • IN • soo • la) — a piece of land almost surrounded by water and connected to a larger body of land
plateau(plat • OH) — an area of elevated flat land
refugee(rehf • yoo • GEE) — one who flees for safety from one country to another
resources(REE • sore • sez) — supplies of materials to use to take care of needs, such as coal or timber
rice paddies(RICE PAD • eez) — fields that are flooded with a few inches of water, used to grow rice plants
scholar(SKAH • ler) — a student with expert knowledge
spirit(SPEER • it) — ghost; fairy or supernatural being
square mile(SKWAIR MYLE) — four-sided area; each side measures one mile; all corners are right angles
tradition(tra • DIH • shun) — an old custom
tribe(TRYBE) — a group of people related by blood and customs
tropical(TROP • ih • kil) — having to do with the parts of the earth just to the south and just to the north of the equator

INDEX

About the Author

Karen Jacobsen is a graduate of the University of Connecticut and Syracuse University. She has been a teacher and is a writer. She likes to find out about interesting subjects and then write about them.